Original title:
A Journey with the Jellyfish

Copyright © 2025 Creative Arts Management OÜ
All rights reserved.

Author: Natalia Harrington
ISBN HARDBACK: 978-1-80587-262-7
ISBN PAPERBACK: 978-1-80587-732-5

Underwater Whispers

In the depths where critters play,
A jelly floats, swaying all day.
With tentacles like spaghetti twirls,
It dances softly, giving swirls.

Tickles and giggles, oh so sly,
It waves to fish that swim on by.
Bubble-blowing jokes it shares,
With gurgles, snickers, and funny airs.

Dance of the Celestial Drifters

In a sea of shimmering light,
Dodging crabs with all its might.
Jelly spins with flair and glee,
A cosmic show for all to see.

Floating free, it's quite the sight,
Turning moonbeams into flight.
Its jiggle makes the anchor crabs,
Chortle loud; it's really fab!

Tentacles and Tides

Waving arms like noodle dreams,
In the currents, laughter streams.
A jelly's plan is quite absurd,
To dance all day without a word.

It twirls through ripples, such delight,
With barnacles that cling too tight.
A ticklish ride on waves so wide,
Where silliness is never shy.

Surreal Voyage through a Liquid Dream

Drifting softly with a grin,
This squishy friend just can't fit in.
With rainbow hues and jelly-jig,
It laughs at creatures, big and dig!

Gliding past a curious shark,
Who finds it strange, a swimming spark.
The ocean's antics never cease,
As jelly floats with blissful peace.

Chasing Phosphorescence

In the twilight's glow, we prance,
A dance with lights, a wiggly chance.
Bubbles giggle, as currents twirl,
Crabby friends in a swirling whirl.

Glimmers flash like stars on the sea,
Tickling faces as we glide with glee.
Jelly's waddle, a comical sight,
We laugh and splash under the moonlight.

Fluid Conversations

Whispers flow like the ocean's breeze,
Bubbly secrets shared with ease.
Tentacles wave with tales to tell,
In this chatty tide, all is well.

With each sway, a giggle escapes,
Wrapping us up in jelly-like drapes.
We trade our jokes in a rippling voice,
In this slippery world, we rejoice.

Timeless Stories Beneath the Surface

Beneath the waves, where time stands still,
Jellies weave stories with a mystical thrill.
Each bob and weave, a plot twist unfolds,
A grand epic of the deep sea holds.

From ancient tales to modern whims,
Their fluid lives are filled to the brim.
As they float past, we can't help but grin,
In this world where the laughter begins.

The Gelid Serenade

In icy depths, we sing our tune,
A frosty jingle, in the light of the moon.
With a jiggle and sway, the jellies prance,
They choreograph the ocean's dance.

Oh, the chill! What a quirky show,
Twisting together as currents flow.
Each icy note, a giggle in air,
With frosty rhythms, we float without care.

Observing Celestial Wanderers

In the depths where blue things glide,
Jelly pals take a wobbly ride.
They wave their tentacles with flair,
Floating like they just don't care.

Bouncing bubbles in the sun's rays,
They dance and shimmer in wild displays.
A jelly trickle, a squishy delight,
Laughing as they drift out of sight.

Chronicles of the Silent Voyagers

Underwater, the misshapen crew,
Wobbling gracefully, they blew.
With no limbs, yet they make a splash,
Floating effortlessly, in a flash.

Whispers of currents guide their way,
Jellyfish plotting a grand ballet.
They giggle as they spin and twirl,
In this azure world, they whirl.

The Glimmering Escape

Glowing softly in the moonlit tide,
Jellybeans dance, oh what a ride!
One tumbled over, with a funny face,
Floating freely, in wobbly grace.

The ocean's laughter fills the air,
As jelly pals flip without a care.
They plot their escape from the seaweed's clutch,
Paddling softly, they vanish—what a touch!

Embracing the Whims of the Sea

In a whirlpool of jelly giggles bright,
They shimmer, they sway, a comical sight.
With each gentle wave, they bend and sway,
Silent jesters of the sea ballet.

They embrace the whims, the playful tide,
Merry mendicants of the ocean wide.
A liver-colored jelly had a funny chat,
With a curious crab, 'What's up with that?'

The Secret Language of Waves

Wobbly friends drift and sway,
Bubbles giggle, bright as day.
Tentacles waving in cheeky glee,
Underwater tales for you and me.

They whisper secrets with every touch,
Floating like clouds, we love them much.
A dance unhinged, both silly and neat,
In the play of currents, oh what a treat!

Embraced by the Ocean's Breath

Slippery glimmers in sunlit beams,
Tickling toes, bursting our dreams.
They hug the shore, our gelatin pals,
Cracking jokes with splashing jowls.

Bobbing along, it's a fishy affair,
Their soft, squishy love fills the air.
With a flick and a swirl, they play hide and seek,
Bubbling laughter, aquatic and chic!

Ethereal Reflections

Mirror-like, they glide so fast,
A glance and a grin, fun none can outlast.
Flickering shadows on bright sandy floors,
Who knew the sea had comedic chores?

With a swish and a flap, they twirl around,
In the depths of the ocean, hilarity found.
No fishy frown here, just jelly joy,
Playing tricks like a mischievous toy!

Unraveling the Sea's Choreography

In whimsical dances, they float with flair,
Jellybeings in suits, bright and rare.
They twirl and they spin, such clumsy delight,
With all of their jiggles, they steal the night.

Crabs clap along in a lively beat,
As we join the beach ball, life's silly feat.
The ocean orchestrates a laugh with its beat,
While jellybeans waddle in giggly retreat!

Beyond the Coral Canopy

In a world of colors bright,
Float they dance, what a sight!
Tentacles wave, so carefree,
Who knew the ocean's a jamboree?

With winkles and jiggly grace,
They wiggle in a playful race.
One took a turn, oh what a blunder,
Belly flops in waves of wonder!

A salty splash, a giggle here,
Who knew the sea held such cheer?
They bubble up like giggling sprites,
Ocean parties on festive nights!

Through coral halls, they prance and glide,
With each bounce, they shift and slide.
In laughter's echo, they align,
Creating joy so divine!

Silent Conversations in the Blue

In hues of turquoise, they convene,
Whispers of jelly in a marine routine.
No words are needed, just a wink,
A funny nudge as they start to sink.

Bobbling softly, they exchange a grin,
Three jelly pals, all set to begin.
With tentacles waving, they share the jest,
Who knew their silence would be the best?

Dancing shadows on the ocean floor,
They chuckle silently, wanting more.
A gurgle here, a plop over there,
In jiggly tales, they banish despair.

So let's dive deep, just for a look,
At these laughter-laden jellyfish with their own book!
In bubbles and giggles, they twist and turn,
In the big blue sea, laughter we yearn!

Embrace of the Tidal Flow

Riding the waves like a tidal twirl,
Jellybeans prance, what a whirl!
They float and flop in a giggly brew,
Who knew ocean life was so askew?

With each wave crest, they bounce and slide,
Side by side, oh what a ride!
Tentacles twine in a bubbly snare,
Rolling laughter fills up the air.

Turned upside down, one lost his cap,
Said, "Oops!" while doing a little flap.
They jive and giggle, oh what a show,
Under the sun's warm, golden glow.

So come and join their tidal play,
Where silliness is the order of the day.
In swirling eddies, they pursue the flow,
Wrapped in laughter, they steal the show!

Soft Emissaries of the Ocean

With bodies like pillows, they softly glide,
In the wavy sea, they laugh with pride.
Gentle squish amid the foam,
Jelly pals call the ocean home.

Tickling currents as they roam,
In search of fun, far from their dome.
They flip and frolic, pure delight,
Turning the tides into sheer highlight.

With glowing charms and goofy spins,
They bobble about on whims and grins.
A jelly jiggle, what a treat,
Spreading giggles with every beat!

So if you spot them, join the fun,
For in this sea, we all are one.
With silly dances and playful cheer,
Soft ocean messengers drawing near!

Translucent Odyssey

In waters bright and clear,
A jelly floated near,
With tentacles like ribbons,
It danced without a fear.

We waved and splashed around,
It swirled without a sound,
Its jellybean-like grace,
Made us giggle and astound.

We chased it in delight,
As it glimmered in the light,
A squishy blur of color,
A pure, whimsical sight.

It slipped between our toes,
A creature everybody knows,
Together we created,
The most hilarious of shows.

Between the Sand and the Sea

Nestled in the sea foam,
A jelly found its home,
With a wink and a jiggle,
It shimmied just to roam.

We built a sandcastle tall,
It slid and made us fall,
With squishy, silly antics,
It entertained us all.

As the tide came and went,
Our laughter was well spent,
That gelatinous darling,
Was quite the mischief-sent!

By sunset's golden glow,
Its glow put on a show,
A funny little critter,
With nowhere else to go.

The Pulse of the Abyss

In the depths of the sea,
A jelly danced with glee,
With pulsating rhythm,
It laughed cheerily.

We joined in the fun,
As bubbles burst, one by one,
This jiggly little monster,
Was a party on the run!

With bright colors aglow,
It sparked ideas to throw,
How to catch its wild waltz,
While letting our smiles grow.

As currents twirled our dreams,
We floated on its beams,
In a hilarious ballet,
That burst at the seams.

Enigmatic Flows

A creature oh-so-fine,
With a shape that's quite divine,
Goes wobbling through the water,
Like jelly on a line.

Its tentacles are quirky,
A sight that's never murky,
We giggled as it jiggled,
In motions slightly jerky.

It drifted to and fro,
In a sea of ebb and flow,
Each pulse a silly dance,
A humor we could show.

With every flap and glide,
We took it in our stride,
This enigmatic wonder,
Bringing joy alongside.

Gliding through the Coastal Veils

In the shallows, I take flight,
With tentacles waving, quite the sight.
Doing somersaults, I twist and spin,
Salty giggles all around, let's begin!

Wobbling along on a current's whim,
I'm the ocean's own playful hymn.
Fish peek out to give a cheer,
'Oh look! The jelly is back here!'

Shimmering in the Depths of Silence

Underwater disco, see me glow,
Bobbing about like I'm in the know.
With a jelly jig and a splashy grin,
Who knew deep blue held this much spin?

The lobsters clap, the crabs take a bow,
Onlookers wonder, 'How does she do that now?'
I'm a floating balloon in the sea's grand hall,
Having a blast, not a care at all!

Unveiling the Ocean's Delicacy

Oh, what a buffet of kelp and foam,
I drift and dine, I call it home.
Seaweed for starters, a jelly delight,
Gourmet meals in the shimmering light!

Squid invite me to a fancy soiree,
With cocktails of brine, a wild buffet.
We toast with bubbles, ha! What a scoop,
As currents groove, we form a troupe!

Portraits of the Deep Blue

Here I float, an artful muse,
With elegant swirls, I choose to cruise.
Fish pose for selfies, eyes open wide,
'Here's a jelly selfie, come surf the tide!'

An octopus painter, oh how he tries,
To capture my grace with ink from the skies.
Yet with a flick, I change my hue,
'Nice try, dear friend, but I'll still outdo you!'

Refuge Beneath the Waves

Floating free with no care,
Tentacles flying in the air.
A pink balloon with quite a grin,
Dodging fish like it's all a win.

Bubbles giggle, laughter rings,
Wobbling here on jelly wings.
Swaying gently, not a fright,
Why fear a splash? It's pure delight!

Who needs a map, or a guide?
Let's just bop with the tide!
We'll snack on plankton, oh so sweet,
In this ocean disco, we can't be beat.

A friend so squishy, weird, and funny,
Makes every wave feel sweet as honey.
With each bob and weave we take,
We find joy in each silly mistake.

The Tidal Embrace

A dance beneath the moonlit glow,
I've got the moves, just so you know.
Slipping, sliding, what a show,
In this marshmallow sea, let's go!

Tangled up, but it's just fine,
My friend and I sip brine and dine.
With a twirl and a flip we sing,
Who knew this was such a fun thing!

Wave after wave, we giggle and glide,
With sparkly critters, we bump and slide.
We bounce like popcorn, up and down,
This ocean party, we wear the crown.

With each splash, our laughter drifts,
In a world where joy just lifts.
Let's make our mark on the salty scene,
As the funniest sea team that's ever been!

Captured in the Drift

Gliding past with style so bold,
A jellyfish's story to be told.
With a wink, it sways like a kite,
Dear jelly, your moves are quite a sight!

Caught in the current, what a thrill,
Jelly giggles, what a silly chill.
In every bubble, a tiny cheer,
As fish flip past with wiggly leer.

Wobbly friends, we share our tales,
Of adventures and wave-riding fails.
Who knew the ocean could be this grand?
With jelly dreams, we swirl hand in hand.

Captured in drift, no need to fret,
Life's better when you're a little wet.
With jelly flair, our spirits rise,
Together we dance 'neath the sea skies.

Dancing Light in the Deep

In the depths where the sunlight plays,
Jelly's swirling in colorful arrays.
With each flicker, a giggle we hear,
A jelly party? Oh my, let's cheer!

Like a disco ball in the blue, so bright,
It spins and twirls under the moonlight.
A glow of fun, a glowing spree,
Who knew that sea life was so zany?

Tentacles wave like ribbons of glee,
This underwater bash is pure jubilee.
We jiggle and jig, as bubbles soar,
Come join the dance, who could want more?

From this watery stage, we put on a show,
With laughter and wiggles, watch us go!
In this jelly ride, let's spread the glee,
A fantastical trip through the deep blue sea!

Celestial Drifters' Serenade

Floating through the ocean blue,
With bobbing heads, they dance and skew.
Twirling, whirling, oh what a sight,
A jelly parade in the moonlight!

Their tentacles wave like silly wands,
As they glide past a band of swans.
"What's that?" they quack with puzzled glee,
"A jellyfish party? Let's join the spree!"

With eyes so wide and grins so bright,
They take a plunge into the night.
Oh, what fun in this wet ballet,
Where jellyfish giggle and splish-splash play!

In a world where currents sway and spin,
These soft floaters surely win.
With every drift a chuckle bloom,
A jellyfish giggle fills the room!

Fluidity of Dreams Below

Beneath the waves where laughter swells,
The jellies weave their merry spells.
With no rigid form to hold them down,
They swirl about like a laughing clown!

Tentacles tickle the shrimp nearby,
As bubbles bubble and fish swim by.
One jelly paused, gave a wink and grin,
"Come join the fun! Let the games begin!"

With a flip and flop, they start to race,
Creating chaos in this vast space.
A splash here, a giggle there,
No worries, just fun, floating in air!

So if you meet them on a briny day,
Just laugh along and join the play.
For deep in the oceans, so vast and wide,
The jellyfish fun is an endless tide!

The Soft Glow of the Depths

In the depths where the dark waters gleam,
The jellies shine like a crazy dream.
Their soft glow brightens the midnight show,
What a sight for all below!

Flipping about like they've lost their mind,
They leave a sparkling trail behind.
"Oh look, it's a disco!" one fish exclaimed,
As the jellyfish waltzed, unashamed!

With colors that dance in the light of the brine,
Those jellies know how to have a good time.
They twirl and swirl without a care,
Brightening the ocean with their flair!

So come let's swim in this glowing spree,
Where laughter echoes from sea to sea.
In the depths, be free, give a jolly cheer,
For jellyfish parties are the best down here!

Luminescent Journeys in the Abyss

In the abyss where the shadows play,
The jellyfish giggle in a carefree way.
With each pulse and twitch, they navigate,
Through the currents of whimsy, they create!

One jelly laughed, "Let's do a flip!"
As they danced a jig on an ocean trip.
All around, in a bubbly sync,
They bounce and bob, just like a wink!

"Who needs a map? We've got our glow!"
Said a jelly with a twirling show.
They drift through waters, so rich and wide,
Crafting stories with each lovely glide!

With a soft chime of laughter in the breeze,
They swirl and giggle with such great ease.
So when you dive where fishtails twirl,
Remember the jellies and let joy unfurl!

The Weightless Waltz

In silken gowns they sway and spin,
A disco ball without a grin.
Tentacles twirl in a carefree breeze,
They dance it out with the utmost ease.

Floating high in the sea's embrace,
Each jelly's step finds a new place.
They wiggle and jiggle, a sight quite rare,
Chasing each other without a care.

A jellyfish spin, oh so absurd,
Like a ballet where no one's heard.
With bubbles popping, laughter flows,
As they pirouette in playful throws.

So let them twirl, these jelly friends,
In weightless jumps that never end.
Their comical dance is quite divine,
In the grand silliness of ocean's shine.

Fluid Fantasies Beneath Waves

Beneath the surf, they're dancing slow,
With jiggly moves that steal the show.
A twist here, a flip and a glide,
Jellybeans of the sea, full of pride.

They bounce and bob in the ocean blue,
Like wobbly balloons, just passing through.
Their gelatin glimmers, a sight to see,
Tickling fish with glee, oh me!

Swimming through dreams, they take a dive,
In a cosmic waltz, they come alive.
Their clear, squishy bodies, a sight to behold,
Turning the sea into laughter untold.

With every sway and playful twirl,
Their jelly giggles make my head whirl.
A bubbly ballet in ocean's sway,
Where fluid fantasies dance all day.

The Submarine Ballet

In the depths where the sea is dark,
Jellyfish glow, each one a spark.
They pirouette in rhythmic raids,
Creating art with their flowing shades.

Underwater, they gracefully glide,
With belly flops and jelly-filled pride.
They slip and slide with a laugh and wink,
In this watery world, they do not stink!

A splash of color, a comedic twist,
Every move's like an oceanist's tryst.
Swirling in currents, a fancy dance,
As squishy stars take their chance.

So here they go, on a jelly spree,
Laughing and leaning with glee so free.
The submarine ballet, a chuckle parade,
In the depths of the sea, fine jokes are made.

Jellywave Reverie

On jellywaves, they ride the tide,
With bobbing heads and nothing to hide.
An undulating giggle, a splash of fun,
Each jellyfish glimmer shines like the sun.

They surf the bubbles, they peek and pop,
A jelly filled party that never stops.
With tentacles waving like ribbons in air,
They pull off tricks with the utmost flair.

Rolling on waves, what a sight to see,
In this jelly-filled fantasy, wild and free.
They slosh and splatter, an oceanic play,
Turning the sea into a jellyfish ballet!

So join the dance in this liquid dream,
Where laughter bubbles and bubbles stream.
With jellywave joy, what a grand view,
In this wacky world where silliness grew.

Encounters with the Enigmatic

On a sunny day, I took a dive,
And suddenly felt quite alive.
Floating by, what a sight!
An umbrella in water, a jelly delight!

With tentacles waving like they were dancing,
I wondered if they were out romancing.
They drifted and twirled, all so abstract,
While I just laughed; that was a fact!

A friendly blob gave me a wave,
I chuckled, 'Hey, thanks for being brave!'
But it turned and swirled, oh what a blur,
Was it shy, or was it a great big spur?

So off they went, my buddies so bright,
Into the blue, they danced with delight.
I waved goodbye with a goofy grin,
Who knew jellyfish could be such a win?

Meditative Musings at Sea

Sitting by the shore, I gazed at the sea,
Wondering what secrets could possibly be.
Then splats of jelly, colors galore,
Drifted by, echoing a marine encore.

With laughter, I watched their comical glide,
As they flopped and flailed, oh what a ride!
Could they be lost? Or just taking a tour?
With each little swirl, I felt the allure.

I pondered their wisdom, so floaty and free,
'Could they teach me how to simply be?'
While they bobbed past, all strange and sublime,
I felt that jelly was keeping good time.

The sun dipped low, casting shadows so long,
And in that moment, I couldn't go wrong.
Playful and silly, they danced in the waves,
Teaching me laughter, oh how it saves!

Transitory Trails of Wonder

Beneath the surface, a world of delight,
Jellyfish boogied, what a strange sight!
Wobbling around without any care,
With squishy round bodies that floated in air.

I tried to mimic their graceful moves,
But tripped on a flipper, oh what grooves!
A jelly flipped over, gave me a glance,
Could it be asking for a jelly dance?

Each wave brought a friend, so silly and sleek,
They giggled and jiggled, oh wouldn't you peek?
With pulsating bells, they played hide and seek,
In their translucent charm, I felt so weak.

As daylight waned and dusk called me near,
Those jelly companions seemed full of cheer.
In watery jest, I waved them goodbye,
Thankful for giggles with creatures that fly!

Embracing the Depths

In the deep blue, where the fishes teem,
Jellyfish floated, living the dream.
Their wobbly forms drifted in style,
As I laughed and leaned in, oh what a while!

With colors that danced in the sunlight's gleam,
They glided and swirled like a wild dream.
I thought, 'Are they lost? Or just feeling vast?'
With each jelly whirl, my troubles flew past.

I tried to converse with a jiggly friend,
It seemed to respond, as if we could blend.
With a bounce and a wiggle, it said, 'Come on, dude!
Life is all squishy, take it in, dude!'

So I spun in circles, joined their delight,
Laughing as jellies twinkled in sight.
With every jelly-like caper and jest,
I found hugging the depths was truly the best!

Ephemeral Elegance

In the sea, they wave so bright,
Drifting in the soft moonlight.
Tentacles sway, oh what a sight,
Making fish jump in pure delight.

Floating by with no great care,
Wearing hats made of seaweed flare.
One gets tangled in a whale's hair,
But they just laugh, it's quite the affair.

Little blobs of jelly cheer,
Bumping boats without a fear.
Capsized sailors shed a tear,
While the jellyfish just giggle near.

They have no worry, they have no rush,
Gliding through the ocean's hush.
If you see one in a plush,
Give a wave, don't be too brusque.

The Ghostly Swirl

In ghostly gowns they dance and twirl,
Underwater, watch them swirl.
Giddy, goofy, a jiggling pearl,
Chasing fish in a crazy whirl.

One floats by with a wink and grin,
As if to say, "Come join the spin!"
A dolphin thinks it's a game to win,
But jelly just laughs, saying, "You'll never begin!"

A sea turtle tried to take a turn,
But got tangled, oh what a burn!
The jellyfish giggle, hearts that yearn,
For every twist, there's a lesson to learn.

In the abyss, they throw a party,
With a style that's far from hearty.
Underwater jokes get a bit naughty,
As they glide by, so light and carty.

Mariner's Lullaby

Sailors hoot under starry skies,
While jelly fish dance, oh how they rise!
They float by like a fun surprise,
Making all the barnacles have wise eyes.

With a flip and a flop, they waltz around,
Tickling toes that grace the ground.
They puff up with giggles, pure joy found,
While sailors on boats barely make a sound.

Oh, how they tease with transparent glee,
Waving hello to each brave mariner spree.
A jelly floats past, then does a spree,
Saying, "Catch me if you can, whee!"

One slips by with a jiggly laugh,
Sailors watch in awe, a slippery craft.
In this sea dance, they find their path,
With jelly smiles that lead to a gasp.

Abyssal Light

In depths where shadows seem to hide,
Jellyfish glow with a vibrant pride.
Bobbing through darkness, side by side,
They throw a party on the tide.

A flicker here, a shimmer there,
Glowing softly, they're everywhere.
They make the crabs stop and stare,
As the sea shimmies without a care.

With lanterns bright, they roam the blue,
Singing songs that sound so new.
Creatures join in, there's quite the crew,
"Dance with me!" they happily coo.

A whale grins, with eyes like stars,
"Join us, friends, forget your scars!"
In this abyss, laughter jars,
As jellyfish lead the fun from afar.

Resinous Reveries

Floating like a balloon, oh so bright,
With tentacles waving, what a sight!
I tried to catch one, but it slipped away,
Dancing in the water, gone to play.

They giggle and glide in their jelly-like glee,
Making a splash, just like me!
With smiles so wide, like they own the day,
I can't help but laugh at their wobbly sway.

Whimsy of the Abyss.

Bobbing and weaving, they're quite the crew,
Wiggly wonders, in shades of blue.
One caught my eye, with a wink and a twist,
I think it just wanted to be on my list!

They sway in the currents, a dance without care,
Wobbling jellybeans, oh, such flair!
I joined their party and spun around too,
What's a little dizzy when you're laughing anew?

Drifting with the Currents

As I float along, a gelatinous dream,
With friends so bizarre, we're a merry team.
They bounce off my head with a squishy delight,
I giggle and gasp—what a comical sight!

Each jiggly move feels like pure delight,
Chasing through bubbles, oh what a flight!
My companions, they shimmer, a glow so divine,
Together we frolic, all tangled in brine.

Embrace of the Ocean's Glow

In the moonlit waves, we sway and collide,
With jellyfish friends, I take in the tide.
We play peek-a-boo under the sea foam,
Each squish and squirm feels just like home.

They giggle in colors, a luminescent cheer,
Each glide through the water brings in the beer!
With laughter like bubbles, we rise and we dive,
These jelly-like jesters make me feel alive!

Floating in the Embrace of the Abyss

In the deep where the giggles swell,
A jellyfish joins the silent yell.
With a bounce and a glow, it's quite the sight,
Floating like a balloon in the darkest night.

Wobbling softly, like a dancing fool,
It twirls 'round seaweed, breaking every rule.
Jelly and fish share a silly dance,
As they sashay through the ocean's expanse.

The currents giggle, the bubbles pop,
A jelly's jiggle makes the sharks stop!
With tendrils like ribbons, swaying in dreams,
It tickles the depths with its playful beams.

In the embrace of the abyss so grand,
Jelly giggles float on like a band.
With each twirl and swirl, joy is released,
A funny ballet from the ocean's east.

Chromatic Choreography

Dancing in colors, like rainbows in motion,
Jellyfish twirl with wild devotion.
A polka dot party, colors galore,
Swirling in laughter, who could ask for more?

They boogie through coral, a sight to behold,
On bubbles they ride, bold tales to unfold.
With a jig here and there, they steal every glance,
Algae and, giggles, they twirl and prance.

A ruckus unfolds in the shimmering blue,
As jelly sways left; it's a laugh-a-thon crew!
Clownfish snicker, pointing and glee,
At the silly jelly, the ocean's marquee.

With a flash of a grin and a bounce in the tide,
These funny friends take the world for a ride.
As waves clap their hands, the ocean's alive,
In the chromatic dance, we all can thrive.

Pulses of the Infinite Blue

In the blue sea's heart, a wobble begins,
With pulsations of humor, where everything spins.
Floats a jelly, all wiggly and round,
With each playful pulse, laughter's unbound.

It frolics in rhythm, no cares in the world,
Around it, the sea life begins to swirl.
With a squeeze and a pulse, it bubbles with glee,
Drawing smiles from fish, both happy and free.

Octopus chuckles, a tickle on a whim,
As jelly flutters, with a swish and a grin.
With soft glowing lights like a starry parade,
In the blue's embrace, it's a saucy charade.

Pulses are laughter, soft waves in delight,
A jelly's jig, a joy to ignite.
In the infinite blue, where the silliness flows,
Every pulse echoes, the fun only grows.

Secrets in the Tentacle Light

In the twilight glow, secrets start to dance,
Jellyfish giggle, giving all fish a chance.
With tentacles flickering, tales to tell,
Underwater whispers, casting a spell.

They sway with the tide, in a luminous show,
A tutus made of light, putting on a glow.
With giggles of bubbles, they peek and play,
As secrets unfold in the ocean's ballet.

A sea cucumber snores, but jellyfish say,
'Come join our shenanigans, come out and stay!'
With each twitch and shimmer, laughter ignites,
In the tentacle light, everyone's alright.

As the moonlight beams, casting stories untold,
The night comes alive, with laughter so bold.
In this watery world, where secrets delight,
Jelly dances with joy, and the stars twinkle bright.

Beneath the Glassy Surface

In waters clear, a dance begins,
With jelly friends, no room for sins.
They float and sway, like silly hats,
As fish look on, and giggle at that.

With tentacles flapping, what a sight,
They twirl and whirl in pure delight.
Bizarre little pals, drifting along,
In a world where they all belong.

Oh, watch them bob like jelly beans,
In a sea of laughter, where joy am gleans.
They tickle the sea with playful grace,
In this bubbly, buoyant, silly place.

So next time you're near, take a peek,
At these wobbly wonders, so unique.
With every splash, a laugh anew,
Beneath the glassy, sparkly blue.

The Art of Gentle Currents

Oh, what a craft, a jelly's art,
They drift and dart like a bubbly cart.
With wobbly moves, they glide with ease,
Making waves that tickle the knees.

Each flap a giggle, each swirl a cheer,
In the gentle currents, joy is near.
They wiggle their way through the ocean's dance,
Inviting all fish to laugh at their prance.

A splash, a flip, how funny they seem,
Stumbling 'round like they're in a dream.
With every push from the currents' sway,
They orchestrate mischief, all through the day.

So if you see them, don't be shy,
Join in the fun, let your spirits fly.
For in this ballet of jelly delight,
Even the seashells start giggling at sight!

Whispering Tides

As waves whisper tales from the sea,
Jellyfish giggle in glee, oh so free.
They jive with the tides, a comical show,
Painting the ocean with laughs in tow.

With a wiggle and jiggle, what a fine sight,
Turning the depths into pure delight.
They dance with the bubbles, a grand parade,
Where all worries fade and laughter's made.

They don't need a compass, just follow the fun,
Drifting along till the day is done.
In a world of smiles, they bob with flair,
Creating a spectacle beyond compare.

So listen close to the sea's soft tune,
A jellyfish yodel, beneath the moon.
With every whisper, they make hearts sing,
In the watery realms, joy's the true king!

Murmurs in the Moonlit Abyss

In the dark depths, where moonlight sails,
Jellies create fun, like tall tales.
With glows of colors, so bright and strange,
They surf the currents, always deranged.

They flounce and bounce, like jelly on toast,
With friends all around, they laugh the most.
Each jelly's a character, quirky and weird,
In the moonlit abyss, joy is cleared.

A flip here, a twirl there, oh what a spree,
They ride on the waves, wild and free.
While sea creatures chuckle, in gleeful delight,
As jellies pop up like balloons in the night.

So take a dive, in the shimmering dark,
Join the fun of the jellyfish park.
For in every murmur and twinkle you see,
Lies a giggle of joy, like honey from bees.

The Serpent of the Sea Foam

In the frothy surf, it glides with grace,
Wobbling wildly, a bubbling face.
It twirls and sways on a drunken spree,
Who knew the ocean held such glee?

With its tentacles flapping like a flailed kite,
It bounces around, what a curious sight!
Chasing the sand, in bubbles it dives,
While the seagulls laugh, oh, what jives!

Its body's a canvas, in colors so bright,
A fluttering rainbow in the moonlight.
"Look at me!" it shouts with a goofy glide,
Turning the tide into a silly ride!

At dawn, it disappears with a wave,
Leaving behind tales, oh, so brave.
A serpent of foam, who's here for fun,
In the ocean's embrace, it's second to none!

Enchanted by the Pelagic Dance

Swaying like a dancer, out in the blue,
It shimmies and sparkles, oh, what a view!
With a jig on the surface, it draws in the fish,
Making them laugh, it's quite the swish!

Tentacles twirling, a wobbly show,
Even the dolphins can't help but glow.
With each little pulse, it draws in a crowd,
Shimmering brightly, oh, it's so loud!

Under seaweed chandeliers, it spins with flair,
Making bubbles and giggles, filling the air.
A ballroom beneath, with no shoes in sight,
As fish twirl around, it's pure delight!

But as night falls, it starts to retreat,
Leaving behind echoes of laughter so sweet.
A dance in the deep, a pelagic spree,
Forever enchanting, as wild as can be!

Legends of the Gelatinous Realm

In waters so deep, where wonders abound,
Lives a jiggly giant, so plump and round.
With a laugh, it jostles, bobbing with cheer,
Telling the tales no one else can hear!

Its gelatin jiggle is famed across seas,
But swim close, and you'll find it's full of cheese!
Legends of bravado that dance in its wake,
As it tells of the squids and sea turtles that shake.

When tempests arise, it laughs like a child,
Spinning and twirling, all carefree and wild.
With each bubble bursting, laughter erupts,
In the heart of the storm, no one ever gets stumped!

Yet with morning's light, it settles once more,
Leaving behind stories of oceanic lore.
A gelatin hero, spinning around,
In the swell of the sea, its joy knows no bound!

Fables of the Tempest

When storms come splashing, so wild and free,
A gelatin fellow swims fearlessly.
With a cascade of bubbles, it rides the wave,
Chasing the winds, what a raucous rave!

Through lightning and thunder, it dances with glee,
Twisting and turning, it's a sight to see.
"Catch me if you can!" it bubbles out loud,
As it makes the rain look ever so proud!

The ocean's a stage, and the jellies parade,
Splashing and dashing, not a moment delayed.
With every tall wave, a comical spree—
Imitating ships, all lost in the spree!

When calm finally comes after tempests have passed,
The laughter of waves brings peace unsurpassed.
But tales of the tempest echo and play,
In the hearts of the jelly, they're here to stay!

Beneath the Waves, a Tale

In waters bright, oh what a sight,
A jiggly friend, dancing in the light.
With bubbles and giggles, a wobbly grin,
We'll sail through the sea, let the fun begin!

Swirling around, with a swish and a sway,
This jellyfish party brightens the gray.
With tentacles waving, it's quite a display,
Who knew the sea could be this cliché?

Beneath the surface, it floats with ease,
Making friends with fish, and teasing the breeze.
A parade of laughter, a whimsical tease,
As corals join in, a colorful spree!

With a giggle and jiggle, we splash and we play,
In a world full of wonders, we shimmer away.
When the tide takes us home, we'll still find a way,
To dance with the jelly, come night or come day!

Glimmers of the Deep

Glimmers shine, like stars in the tide,
With jelly friends, we take a ride.
Bouncing along with colors so bright,
A touch of the sea, a splash of delight!

In the deep's embrace, oh what a tease,
Our gelatinous pals dance with the breeze.
They bubble and wobble, with laughter that frees,
Who wouldn't join in this underwater freeze?

Curly and swirly, they float in a line,
Swaying the currents, oh look, they're divine!
With whimsy and charm, they steal the sunshine,
A spectacle joyous, an aquatic design!

The ocean's a stage, let the humor unfold,
As jellyfish juggle pearls, bright and bold.
With each little wiggle, our treasures are sold,
In the belly of the sea, to laughter we're told!

Unraveling Sea Mysteries

Underwater secrets, so strange and grand,
With jellyfish winks, they take our hand.
A riddle of ripples, a curious band,
Jumping through waves, it's all unplanned!

With tentacles dancing, a puzzling spree,
What joys lie hidden beneath the sea?
A tickle, a giggle, a flutter, whee!
In the heart of the ocean, wild and free!

Silly and squishy, they float like a kite,
Through magic encounters, they bring pure delight.
Each twist tells a tale, a giggly bite,
In a world of wonders, day turns to night!

Jelly's whimsical ways, oh what a sight,
Unraveling mysteries, full of sheer might.
In the pulse of the sea, where laughter ignites,
With jelly friends close, adventure feels right!

Chasing the Celestial Drift

In moonlit waters, we glide and drift,
With jelly companions, a quirky gift.
Tickled by starlight, we wiggle and twist,
With laughter and joy, how could we resist?

Each glide through the depths, a whimsical dance,
Sprinkling joy with every chance.
They swirl like rainbows, in a sea of romance,
INVITE the world to join this prance!

Diving through dreams, on waves that uplift,
Jelly makes giggles, a marvelous gift.
In pursuit of the cosmos, where wonders sift,
Together we wander, with spirits so swift!

As currents carry tales from the past,
We laugh at the memories, forever to last.
With jellyfish magic, our hearts beat fast,
In the sea of the stars, our dreams are cast!

Whispers in the Currents

Beneath the waves, all is bright,
A jelly dances, what a sight!
It floats along like a balloon,
While fish giggle, singing a tune.

Tentacles waving, oh so free,
Tickling fish, it's pure glee!
With a swirl and a flip, it glides,
In the ocean's playful tides.

A jelly's got style, that's for sure!
With jelly moves, so quirky and pure.
Bubble-blowing with fish as a team,
Together they form an aquatic dream.

So if you catch a glimpse one day,
Of a jellyfish letting loose at play,
Just laugh along, don't be shy,
In the sea's fun, we all can fly.

Dancing in the Moonlit Tides

Under the moon, the waters gleam,
A jelly sways, like in a dream.
With every pulse, it takes the floor,
While seaweed waltzes, asking for more.

Clownfish giggle as they swim,
Join the jelly's disco whim.
With lights aglow, they spin and twirl,
As crabs snap-claw in a silly swirl.

Jelly's rhythm is quite a sight,
Bouncing round in sheer delight.
It shows off moves that make you grin,
With every jig, it pulls you in.

So if you're feeling blue and lost,
Just watch the jelly, no matter the cost.
For in those tides, under a bright moon,
You'll find joy that makes you swoon.

Floating Through Aquatic Dreams

In the blue depths, jelly reigns,
Floating light, no earthly chains.
With a pop and a bounce, it drifts with ease,
While seahorses giggle, catching the breeze.

Tentacles trailing, a ribbon of fun,
Waving hello to everyone.
It spins a tale of delightful bliss,
As fish swim close and steal a kiss.

With each movement, it paints the sea,
Creating a dance, oh so free!
Bubbles burst, laughter unfolds,
Jelly's joy is worth more than gold.

So float along with our jelly friend,
Where whimsy and laughter never end.
In these aquatic dreams, you'll find a way,
To brighten up any dull day!

A Voyage Beneath the Sea

Sailing through the waves, what fun,
A jelly's adventure has just begun!
With bubbles trailing like confetti,
The ocean's stage is always ready.

Schools of fish all gather 'round,
For a jelly show, a splashy sound.
As sea stars clap with arms held high,
A giggle floats up to the sky.

Jelly spins, it's a sight to behold,
With moves that make it quite bold.
In every nook of the briny deep,
Jelly brings joy that we all can keep.

So take a dip, don't miss the spree,
Join our jelly in wild jubilee.
Under the waves, let laughter be,
In this ocean of pure, silly glee.

The Ethereal Sea Nomads

In the wave's soft embrace they glow,
Drifting along with barely a row.
Tentacles dancing, a whimsical sight,
They giggle in bubbles, oh what a flight!

With glee, they hitch rides on the backs of the fish,
Dining on plankton, their fanciful dish.
Crowned in the tides, they're wearing a frown,
Yet keep swooping low like they own the town!

A swirl of colors, in hues so bright,
These nomads of jelly bring pure delight.
While seagulls squawk, they roll their eyes,
"Oh please, we're way cooler," they wagglily rise!

With each squishy pulse, they skirt through the foam,
A parade of jello beneath the sea dome.
Who knew that the ocean had such a crew?
The jellyfish jesters not shy, but askew!

Navigating the Depths of Light

Beneath the surface where sparkles ignite,
Our jelly pals float, what a marvelous sight!
Mapping the currents, like cartographers bold,
With a wave of their arms, stories unfold.

They twirl through the bubbles, like dancers in glee,
Experts in laughter, oh so carefree!
With each little jiggle, they send out a flair,
"Watch out, fellow fish, we're the team without care!"

They play hide and seek with a curious shark,
"Catch us if you can!" they giggle and spark.
With a swish and a swirl, they leap, bounce, and play,
Leaving creatures bewildered along the way.

In the depths of light, their fun never wanes,
Bouncing off corals like jellyfish trains.
A shimmering party, swirling all night,
With each flicker of goo, they spread pure delight!

Moonlit Compositions

Under the moonlight, they waltz without care,
Gliding so smoothly, in silky moon hair.
They write their own tunes in the soft ocean sway,
"Who knew we could compose!" they joyfully play.

The stars twinkle brightly, a concert so fine,
With seaweed as violins, they intertwine.
Their melodies bubble, a whimsical beat,
A fanciful jam that can't be beat!

As dolphins look on, they can't help but grin,
The jellyfish symphony, ready to begin.
With tentacles waving, they lead the parade,
In the moonlit ballroom, where fun is displayed.

So join in the fun, for the night's not yet done,
With laughter and jiggles, they bask in the sun.
These jellyfish maestros, crafty and spry,
Creating pure magic beneath the night sky!

The Silken Path of the Sea

On the silken paths, they gracefully glide,
With giggles and jigs, they take sea in stride.
Painting their trails in ephemeral hues,
With laughter as bubbles, they dance and snooze.

They flirt with the currents, a playful tease,
Riding the waves with the utmost ease.
"Oh look at us, masters of flair!"
They twinkle their charms, without a care.

With every soft pulse, they ripple through time,
Making new friends, oh, what a rhyme!
Waving to turtles, they swirl and they bounce,
In this underwater shindig, fun's in every ounce.

So come join this frolic, the sea's silly jest,
With jellyfish laughter, life is the best.
In the silken sea paths, let your troubles be few,
For dancing with jellyfish is what we must do!

Secrets in the Saltwater

Beneath the waves where critters swish,
A jelly floats, as smooth as a dish.
It tickles fish with its silky trails,
While crabs just roll their eyes and wail.

Gliding gracefully, oh what a sight,
Wobbly friends in moonlit night.
When a wave knocks, watch them dance,
All swaying together in a silly trance.

They giggle and wiggle, so carefree,
While barnacles laugh, sipping their tea.
Slime-coated boogers in a deep sea ball,
Dodging each splash, they're having a ball!

Waving goodbye to the passing squid,
Our bubbly pals keep dancing, undid.
With glowing laughter, they float on by,
In their secret world, where strange critters lie.

Radiance of the Forgotten Deep

In the blue abyss where shadows creep,
Luminous blobs make fish leap.
Jelly giggles sparkle and shine,
Making all sea creatures entwine.

Bobbing like balloons in the ocean's breeze,
Tickling turtles, no one's at ease.
Mysterious forms like floating kites,
Drawing in sailors with their silly sights.

A disco party in the midnight sway,
With jelly friends leading the way.
Each swish and swirl is a merry parade,
In the depths below, where legends are made.

Fishy grins and playful splashes,
While jellybeans glide, oh how time dashes!
They sing to the stars, a bubbly song,
As creatures below tap along all night long.

Flowing Spirit of the Sea

The ocean whispers, secrets unfold,
With jellies spinning tales, oh so bold.
They twirl and swirl in a zany quest,
While curious critters laugh and jest.

A flinging tentacle here, a wiggly spin,
Bizarre ballet where the fun begins.
As dolphins dive, they join the spree,
In this slippery, silliness, wild and free.

Flip, flap, and flop, such a delightful scene,
Bright colors waltzing in a marine routine.
They circle and frolic, a jelly parade,
Chasing the waves where the sea grass swayed.

In the splashes of salt, giggles ignite,
Floating companions through day and night.
Together they swirl, a dreamlike delight,
Guided by laughter, oh what a sight!

The Eternal Float

Floating forever, a jellyfish dream,
With a bounce and a wiggle, it joins the stream.
Tickling the coral, with not a care,
In the dance of the ocean, no worries to bear.

A flutter here, a shimmer there,
With every swirl, they fill the air.
Crustaceans join in with snapping claws,
In the jelly's wake, there are laughs and guffaws.

Oceans of bubbles, stories unfold,
As currents carry secrets of old.
The jellies giggle, a conspiratorial crew,
In the vast, wild sea, they're never blue.

On tides of joy, they drift in delight,
With glowing bodies in the dusky night.
An eternal float with friends far and wide,
In the whimsical waters, they'll always glide.

Serpentine Love Letters from the Sea

Oh, the jelly, so squishy, wafting by,
With tentacles swirling like a dance in the sky.
It whispers sweet nothings, oh what a tease,
Invertebrate flirts, bringing us to our knees.

The ocean's a letter, penned in soft swirls,
Where jellyfish giggle and give us their twirls.
With stings of affection, they float to the beat,
A love song of bubbles, oh isn't it sweet?

That time in the tide, when I tripped on my shoe,
The jelly looked at me, as if saying, "Boohoo!"
We laughed at the sand, as it sprayed on my face,
An awkward romance in a jellyfish place.

So here's to the squishies, the drifters, the glee,
With letters of laughter, they dance just for me.
A waltz with the waves, a caress from the foam,
My heart is a jelly, in the sea we call home.

Echoes of Ethereal Creatures

In waters so clear, where the jellyfish glide,
With pulsating bellies, they swish and they slide.
They hold court in currents, all regal and bright,
Echoing laughter in the cool ocean night.

Floppy and floaty, they bob with great flair,
Each sway a soft giggle from the ocean's own chair.
They sneak up and jive, give a squishy surprise,
With their graceful antics, how we roll our eyes!

"Look there!" I exclaimed, "Check that one out, see?"
As a jellyfish twinkles, like it's winking at me.
But just as I pointed, it gave me a splash,
A slippery cheeky, giggling jelly dash!

So let's raise a toast to these creatures so funny,
With their jiggly jiggles and antics so punny.
They wink from the depths, all aglow in the blue,
In the echoes of laughter, we splash back at you.

Threads of the Celestial Sea

In the depths of the blue, where the squishy ones play,
They write yarns of mischief in their own funny way.
Threads of soft laughter, here, there, and around,
Jellyfish weaving joy from the waves that abound.

With each little ripple, they trip on a wave,
Tickling the fishes as they somersault brave.
A tapestry fun, made of jelly-like smiles,
We swim through the ocean, laughing all the while.

They float by us, winking, like stars in a dance,
Every pulsating jig, a giggly romance.
Those threads of the sea, we pull tight with a grin,
With jellyfish capers, it's a party we're in!

So let's knit a story, of blunders and glee,
With threads made of jelly and bubbles of spree.
In the celestial tide, we'll twirl and we'll flip,
With squishy companions, we'll sail on this trip.

Chasing Bioluminescent Dreams

In the dark midnight waters, we chase glowing gleams,
Jellyfish dancing like stars in our dreams.
They flicker like candles on a mystical stream,
As we giggle and glide, in a playful regime.

Oh, the glow of their bodies, a sight to behold,
Like neon-lit lanterns, they shimmer and fold.
With each wobbly wave, they guide us with cheer,
In this oceanic circus, we've nothing to fear.

A jelly did somersault, laughing all the way,
Spinning brighter than fireworks—oh what a display!
But just as I reached for that shimmering flash,
I slipped on a shell, and into the splash!

Yet in that warm water, we buoyantly swayed,
With jellyfish giggles, our worries allayed.
So let's chase the night, with dreams made of light,
In the bioluminescence, we dance till it's bright.

www.ingramcontent.com/pod-product-compliance
Lightning Source LLC
Chambersburg PA
CBHW070321120526
44590CB00017B/2769